# GOOD NEWS of Great Joy!

*by Sally Michael*

**ILLUSTRATIONS BY: NICOLE MANUEL**

**Truth:78**

*Good News of Great Joy*
By Sally Michael

Our vision at Truth78 is that the next generations know, honor, and treasure God, setting their hope in Christ alone, so that they will live as faithful disciples for the glory of God.

Our mission is to inspire and equip the church and the home for the comprehensive discipleship of the next generation.

We equip churches and parents by producing curriculum for Sunday School, Midweek Bible, Intergenerational, Youth, and Backyard Bible Club settings; vision-casting and training resources (many available free on our website) for both the church and the home; materials and training to help parents in their role in discipling children; and the Fighter Verses™ Bible memory program to encourage the lifelong practice and love of Bible memory.

Copyright © 2021 Next Generation Resources, Inc. Illustrations Truth78. All rights reserved. No part of this publication may be reproduced in any form without written permission from Truth78.

Published in the United States of America.

ISBN: 978-1-952783-41-8

Toll-Free: (877) 400-1414
info@Truth78.org
Truth78.org

All Scripture quotations are from The Holy Bible, English Standard Version® (ESV®). Copyright © 2001 by Crossway, a publishing ministry of Good News Publishers. Used by permission. All rights reserved. ESV Text Edition: 2016.

**Truth:78** / Equipping the Next Generations to Know, Honor and Treasure God

Truth78.org · info@Truth78.org · (877) 400-1414 · @Truth78org

# A NOTE TO PARENTS

This book is a companion to *Good News of Great Joy Family Advent Calendar and Readings,* published by Truth78. As such, it can be used in several ways:

- As a resource for a very young child in the family who will need help understanding the main point of the Bible reading for the day.

- As a review of key points and facts of the daily Bible passages. You might choose to do only the section corresponding to the daily reading, or you might choose to review previous pages either by reading parts of the text or by talking about the content using your own wording.

- If you have no older children and will not be reading the Scripture portion or only part of the Scripture portion on the Advent calendar cards, you could choose to use the book as the main teaching tool and reveal the calendar cards each day.

However you decide to use the book, we recommend reading just one section each day. Look at the picture with your child. Read the words, stopping to explain any words or concepts your child does not understand. Discuss the biblical truths and work of God revealed in the text. Pray with your child. Your child can then reveal the picture on the calendar for the day.

If you are also reading the Scripture portions in the *Family Advent Calendar and Readings* with children in the family, you could follow up with the corresponding pages in this book, or you could start with the pages in this book and then do the corresponding readings in the *Family Advent Calendar and Readings*. You may want to quickly review the main point of previous pages as you continue along in the book. The book and calendar content can also be reviewed using the *Good News of Great Joy Coloring Book*.

This book can be used alone or alongside the *Good News of Great Joy Family Advent Calendar and Readings* as well as a related coloring book. It is not intended to be read through in one sitting. Ideally, it is to be used as a daily Advent devotional by reading and discussing the sections for the corresponding dates in December.

# RIGHTEOUS

## December 1
## A Childless Couple

Meet Zechariah and Elizabeth. They look like a grandma and a grandpa, don't they? But they aren't. They don't have any grandchildren . . . They don't even have any children! They had prayed many years for a child. But Elizabeth never had a baby. Now she was too old.

---

**Luke 1:5-10**

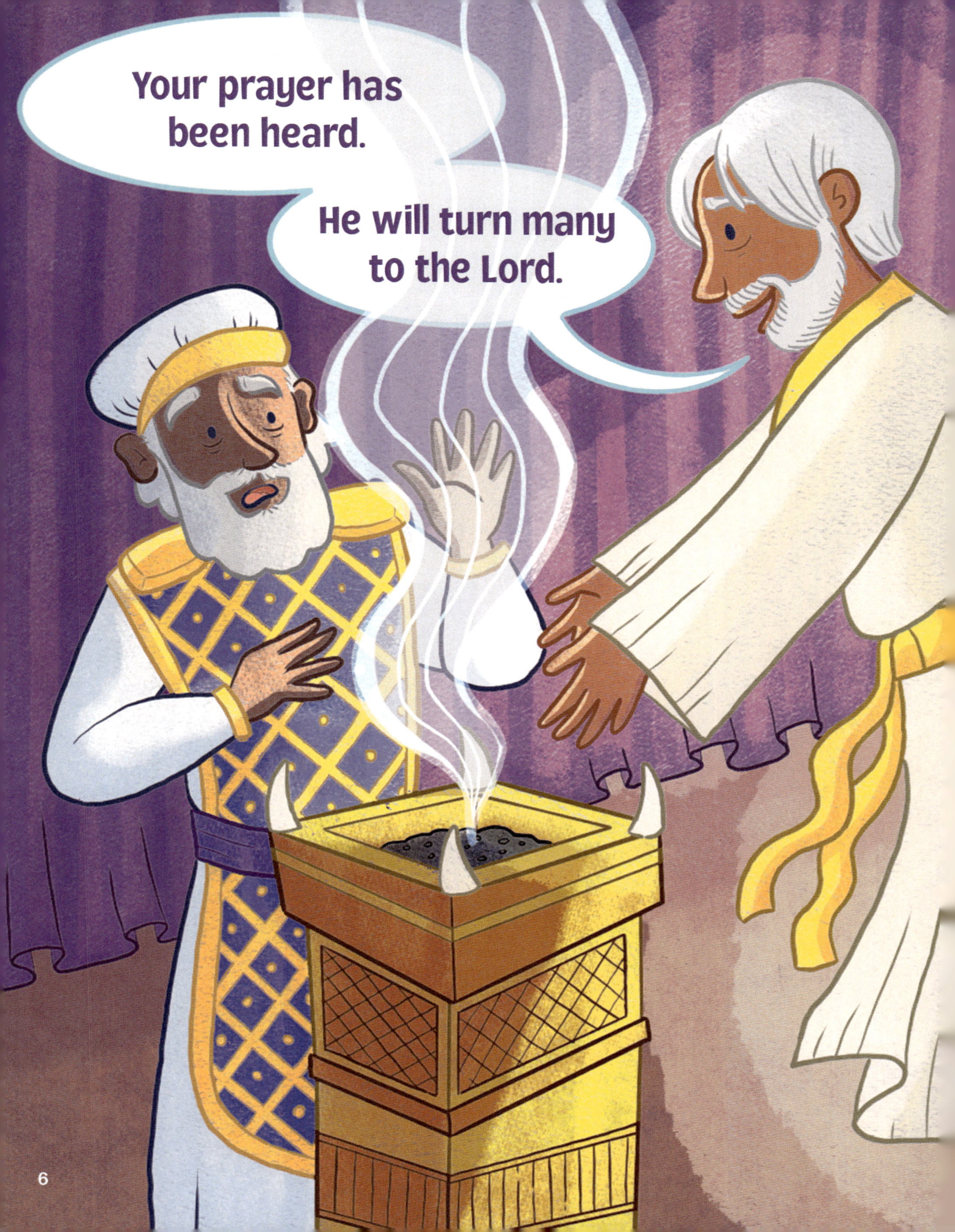
Your prayer has been heard.
He will turn many to the Lord.

## December 2
# A Message for Zechariah

Zechariah was a priest. He worked in the temple. One day when he was working in the temple, something very surprising happened! An angel came to Zechariah with a message: *"Your prayer has been heard."* Zechariah and Elizabeth were going to have a baby boy! His name would be John.

But that's not all the angel told Zechariah. There was even better news! Their baby John would grow up to *"be great before the Lord."* He would be God's messenger! He would tell people to get their hearts ready because . . . an *even more special Person* was coming!

Luke 1:11-20

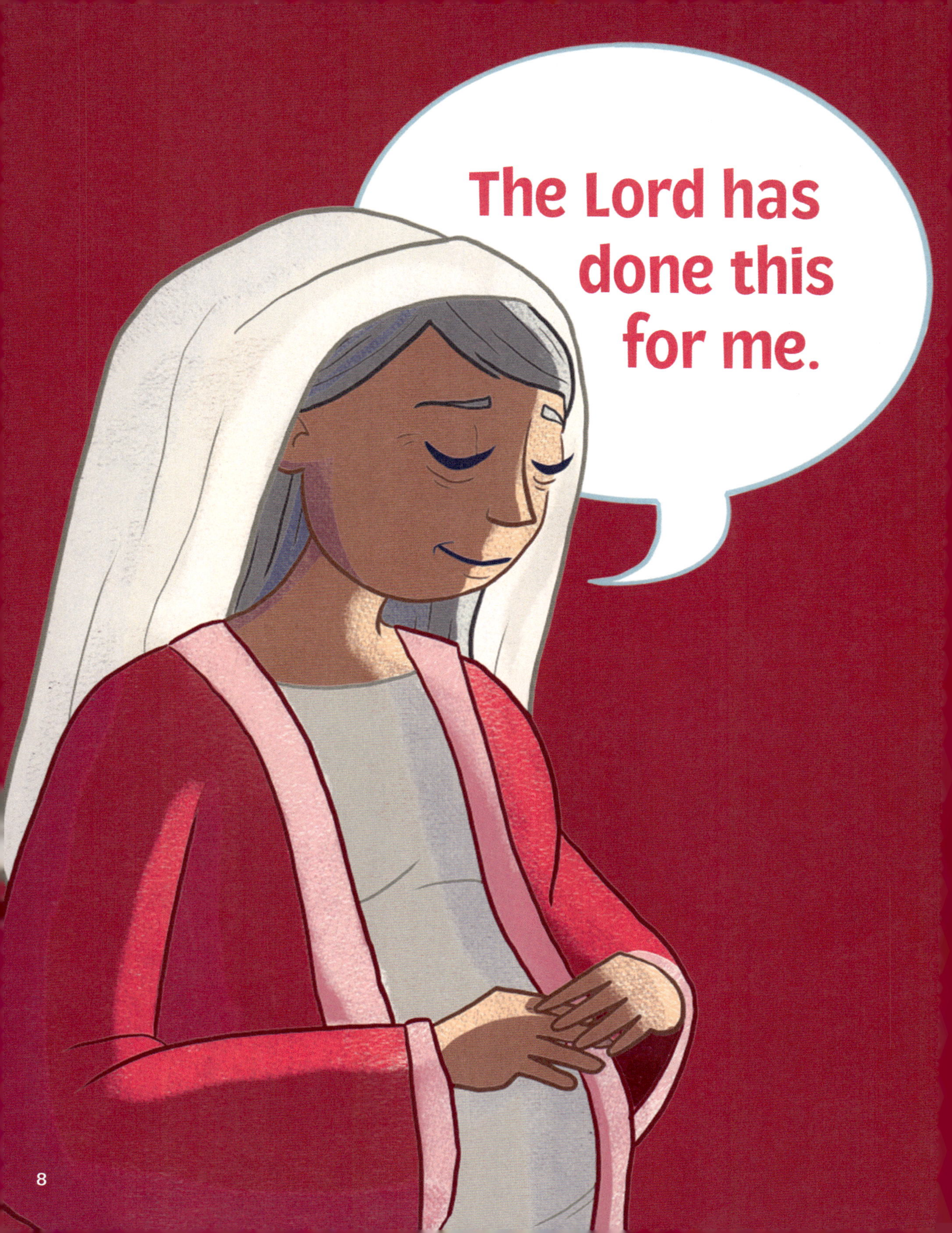
The Lord has done this for me.

## December 3
# GOD BLESSES ELIZABETH

How could Elizabeth have a baby? She was too old to have a baby. But nothing is too hard for God. Soon there was a baby growing in Elizabeth's belly! She was carrying the baby who would grow up to bring the news about the *even more special Person.*

---

**Luke 1:21-25**

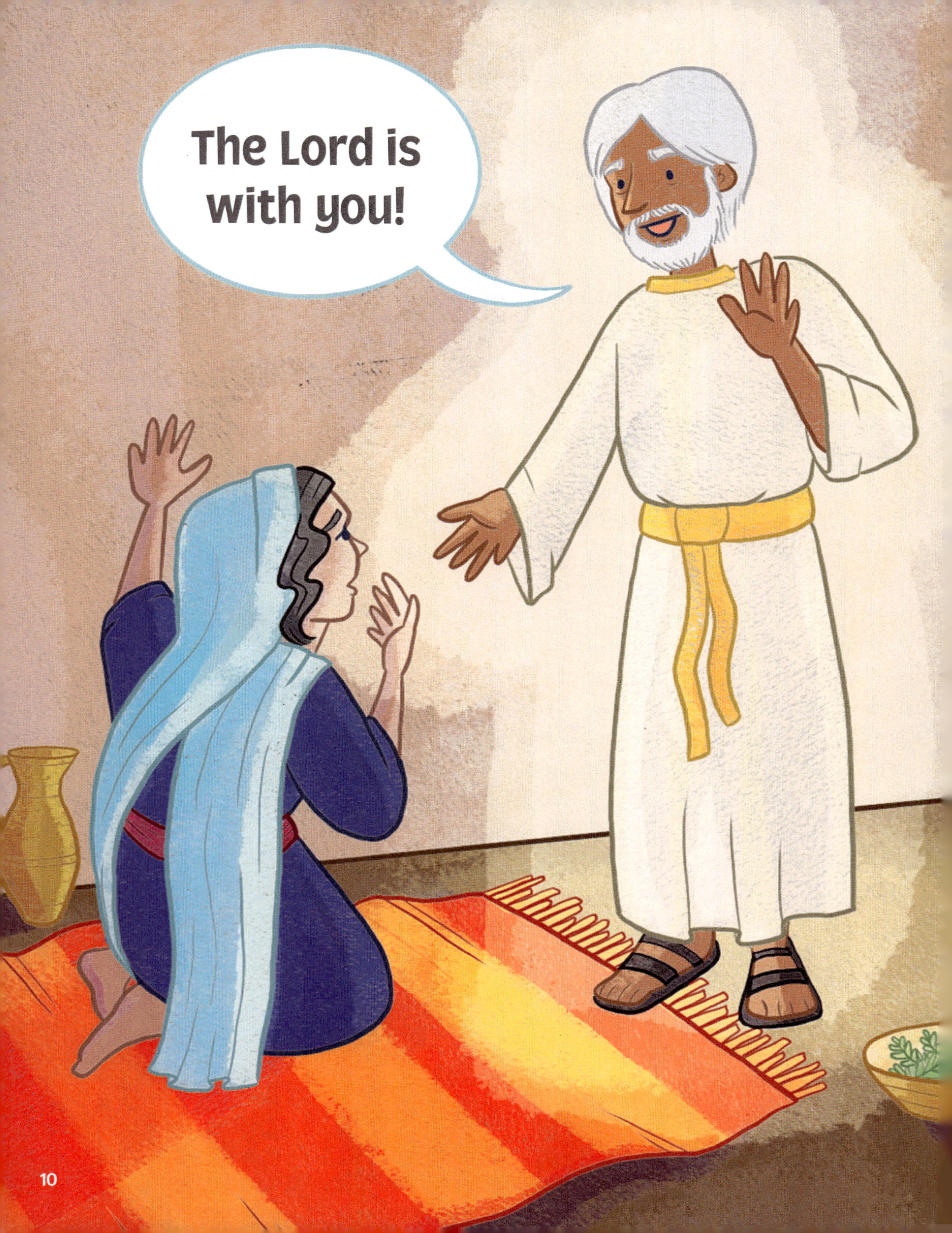
The Lord is with you!

## December 4
## A MESSAGE FOR MARY

Who was this special Person? An angel came with *another message* about *another baby.* This time, the angel came to a young lady. Her name was Mary, and she lived in Nazareth. The angel told Mary, *"The Lord is with you!"* Mary would have a baby. Her baby would be named Jesus, and He would be the Son of the Most High! God's very own Son! This was the *very special Person* who was coming!

---

Luke 1:26-33

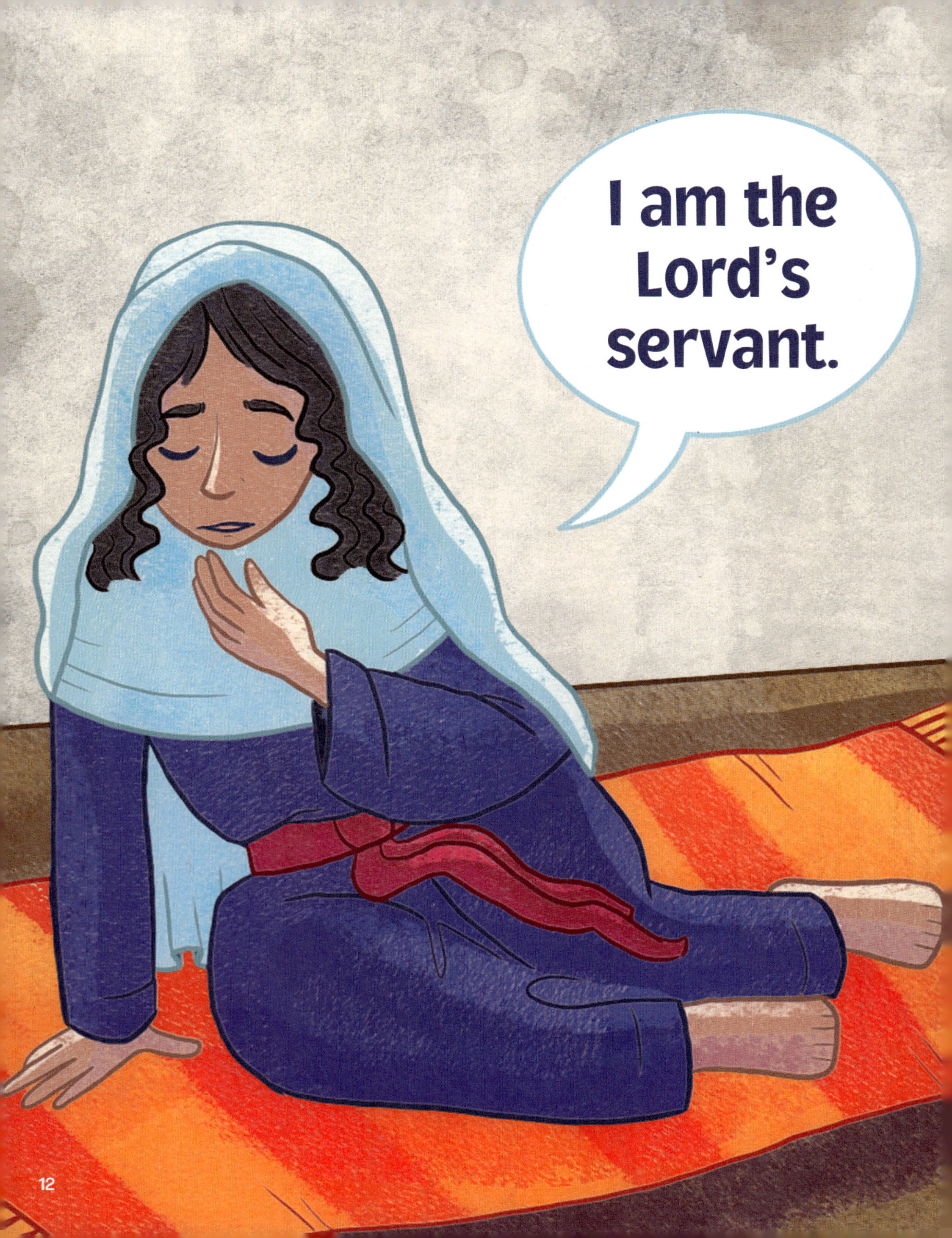
I am the Lord's servant.

## December 5
## MARY WILL BEAR GOD'S SON

This might be a problem for Mary. She was supposed to marry Joseph and have *his* children. But *now*, she would have God's Son. What would Joseph think? Would he be glad, or sad, or even mad?

And how could Mary have a baby? How could she have God's Son? All of this sounded impossible! But nothing is too hard for God! God had already done something impossible. The angel told Mary that God was giving old Elizabeth a baby. *For nothing will be impossible with God.*

So Mary said, *"I am the servant of the Lord."* Mary wanted to do what God said. She would be the mother of Jesus.

---

Luke 1:34-38

14

*December 6*
# Elizabeth's Baby Leaps for Joy

God was bringing two special babies into the world! Mary hurried to see Elizabeth. When Mary saw Elizabeth's big belly, Mary believed what God had told her. Elizabeth really was going to have a baby! Just like God promised!

When Mary spoke to Elizabeth, the baby in Elizabeth's belly jumped for joy! Then Elizabeth knew that Mary's baby really was God's Son. This was such good news!

What did Mary do? Mary worshiped God—she told God how great He is! *"My soul magnifies the Lord, and my spirit rejoices in God my Savior."*

---

### Luke 1:39-46
Additional Reading: Luke 1:47-56

# JOHN

## The Prophet of the MOST HIGH

*December 7*

# THE PROPHET OF THE MOST HIGH IS BORN

One day, Elizabeth began to feel some pains. Her baby was coming! Would it be a baby boy? Yes! It was a boy . . . just like God's angel had said. Their friends and family were so excited when they heard the news! They were so happy! God had been very good to these two old people.

Elizabeth and Zechariah named the baby John. Then Zechariah praised God: *"Blessed be the Lord God . . . for he has visited and redeemed his people."* John would be God's messenger. He would tell the people about the Savior who would come to save His people from their sins.

---

**Luke 1:57-58, 62-64, 67-70, 76-77**

Additional Reading: Luke 1:57-80

18

## December 8
## A MESSAGE FOR JOSEPH

What about Mary's baby? When Joseph found out that Mary was going to have a baby, he was *not* excited. Whose baby was this? Who was the father? Joseph knew he wasn't the father. Maybe he would not want Mary to be his wife now.

But God sent an angel to Joseph in a dream. The angel had *another* message. He told Joseph not to be afraid. Joseph should take Mary to be his wife. Mary's baby was truly the Son of God.

---

Matthew 1:18-20

# God With Us
# Jesus
### He will save his people from their sins.

## December 9
# AN ANGEL FORETELLS THE BIRTH OF JESUS

This was wonderful news! God had promised many, many years ago that He would send His Son to be born as a baby. And now God was keeping His promise! God's Son, Jesus, would save His people from their sins!

---

**Matthew 1:21-25**

# ABRAHAM

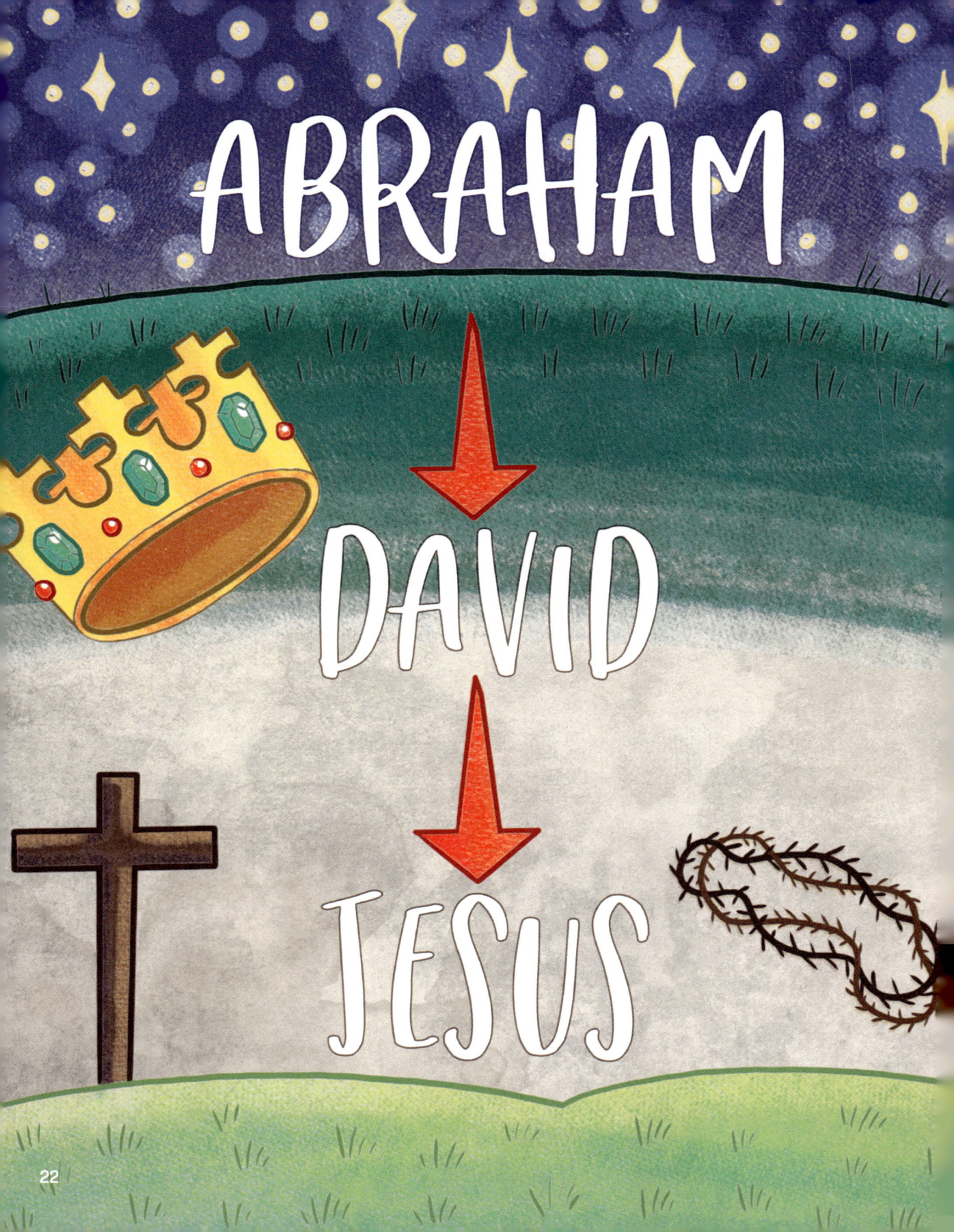

↓

# DAVID

↓

# JESUS

## December 10
## Jesus, a Son of Abraham

Long ago, God had promised to give Abraham a child, grandchildren, great-grandchildren... a whole family of many people would come from Abraham. King David was part of this great family of Abraham. But the most important, most wonderful Person of the many, many people in Abraham's family would be Jesus, the Savior.

---

**Genesis 12:1-3; 15:5-6; Matthew 1:1**
Additional Reading: Matthew 1:2-17

24

## December 11
# A King's Decree

Joseph believed God and took Mary to be his wife. Just before this special baby was born, a new law was made. Everyone had to go to the town they were from to be counted. Joseph and Mary would have to travel to Bethlehem.

―――――――

**Luke 2:1-3**

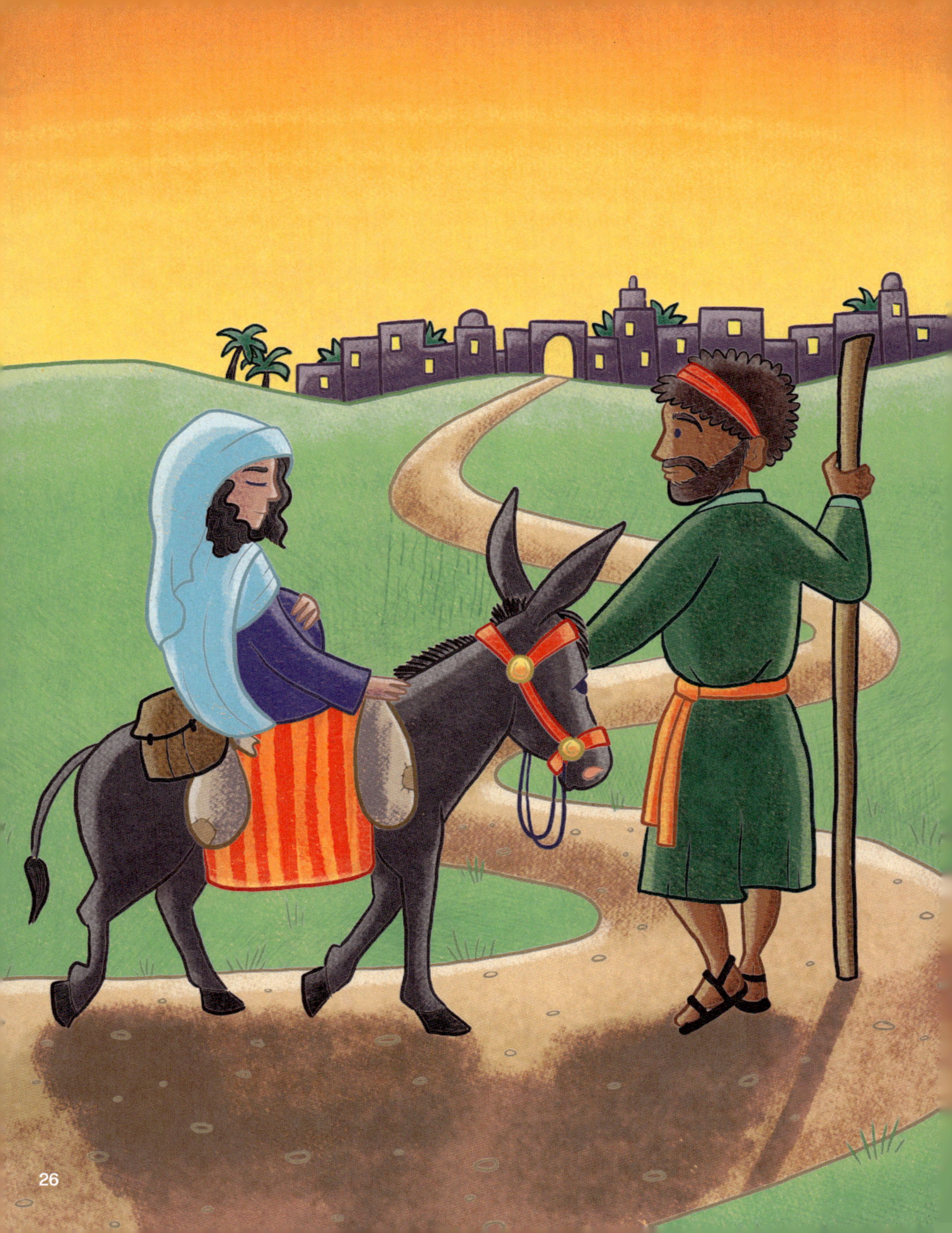

## December 12
# BETHLEHEM: A PROPHECY FULFILLED

What a long trip this would be for Mary, who was almost ready for her baby to come. Why did they have to go to Bethlehem now? Was this a mistake? Didn't God know that Jesus was going to be born soon?

God knows everything! And He never makes a mistake! A long time before Jesus was born, God had said that the Savior would be born in Bethlehem, not in Nazareth where Joseph and Mary lived. When God says that something will happen, it always happens.

---

**Micah 5:2; Luke 2:4-5**

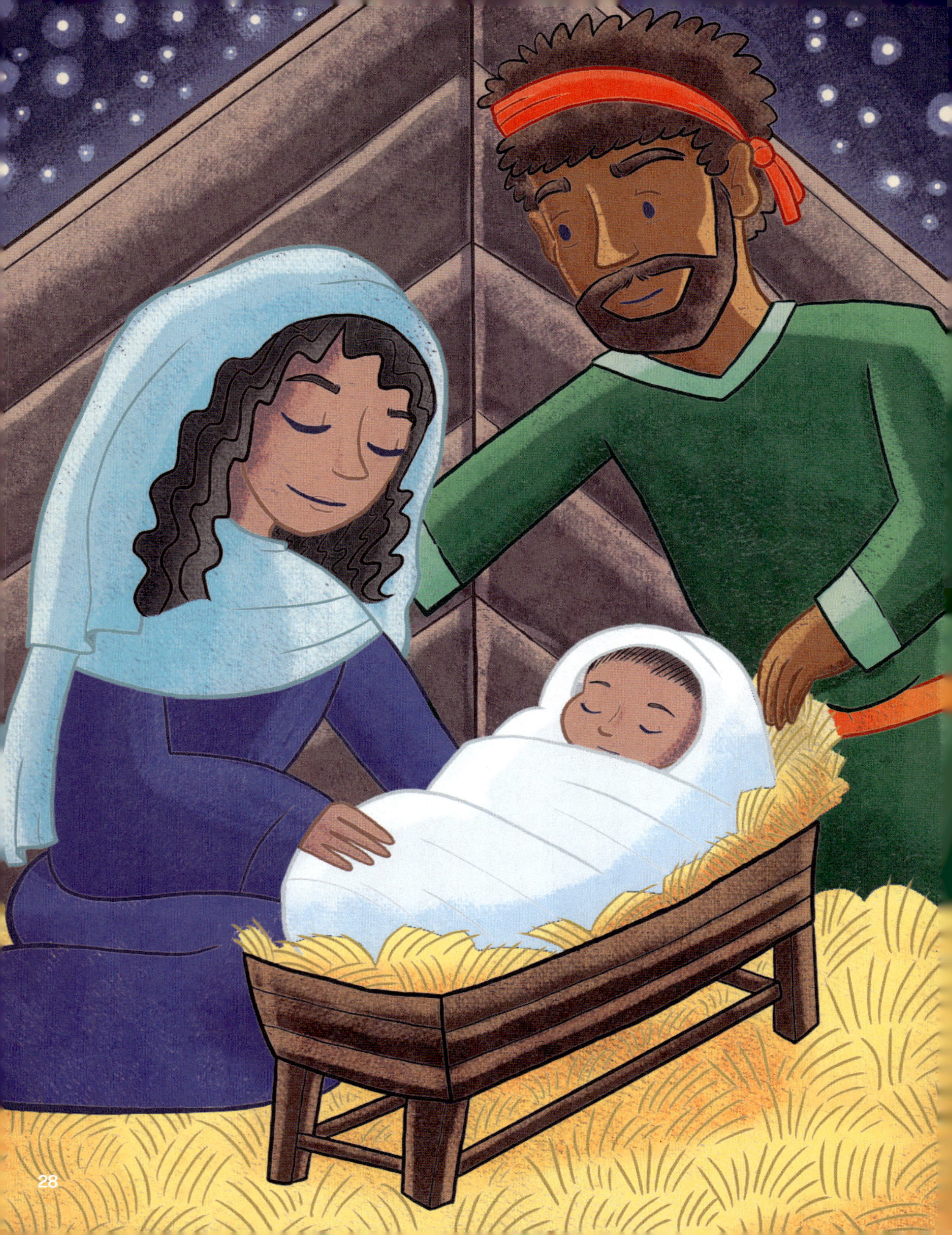

## December 13
# The Birth of Jesus

Off to Bethlehem went Mary and Joseph. And right there in Bethlehem Jesus was born . . . just as God had promised. God's Son wasn't born in a fancy hotel or a palace. He wasn't even born in a house. He was born where the animals were kept. He didn't have a crib. He slept in a manger, a box for the cows' food.

Was this baby in the manger really God's Son? The Son of the Most High?

---

Luke 2:6-7
Sing: "Away in a Manger"

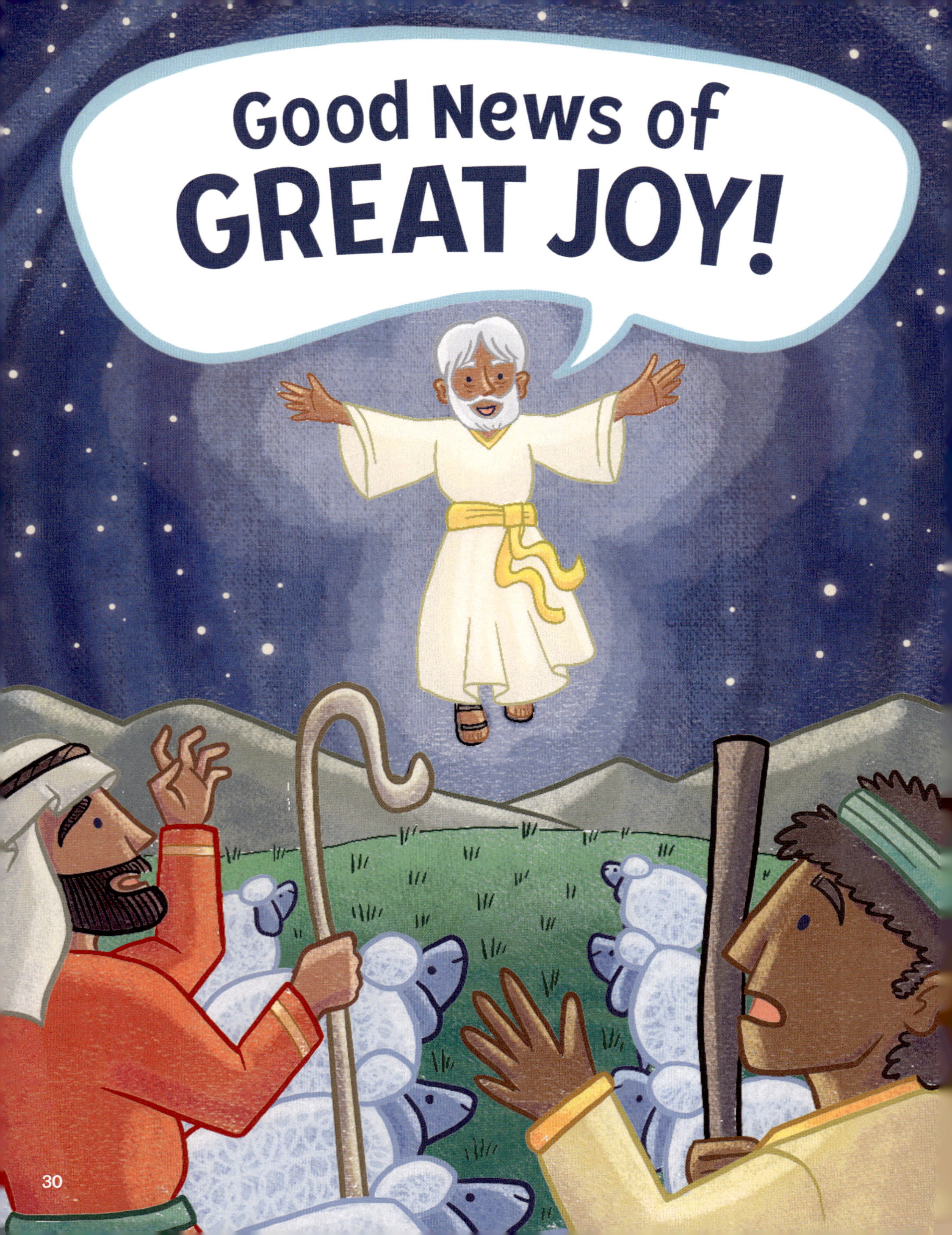
Good News of
GREAT JOY!

## December 14
# The Shepherds Hear Good News!

Who would be awake on this special night? There were shepherds in a field watching their sheep. It was dark, and they were probably very tired. But good shepherds must keep their sheep safe from wild animals . . . hour after sleepy hour.

Suddenly the dark sky was bright! What was happening? Light was shining all around! Then the shepherds saw an angel! Oh, how scared they must have been! But the angel said, *"Fear not, for behold, I bring you good news of great joy that will be for all the people. For unto you is born this day in the city of David a Savior, who is Christ the Lord."*

---

Luke 2:8-12

A Savior is born!

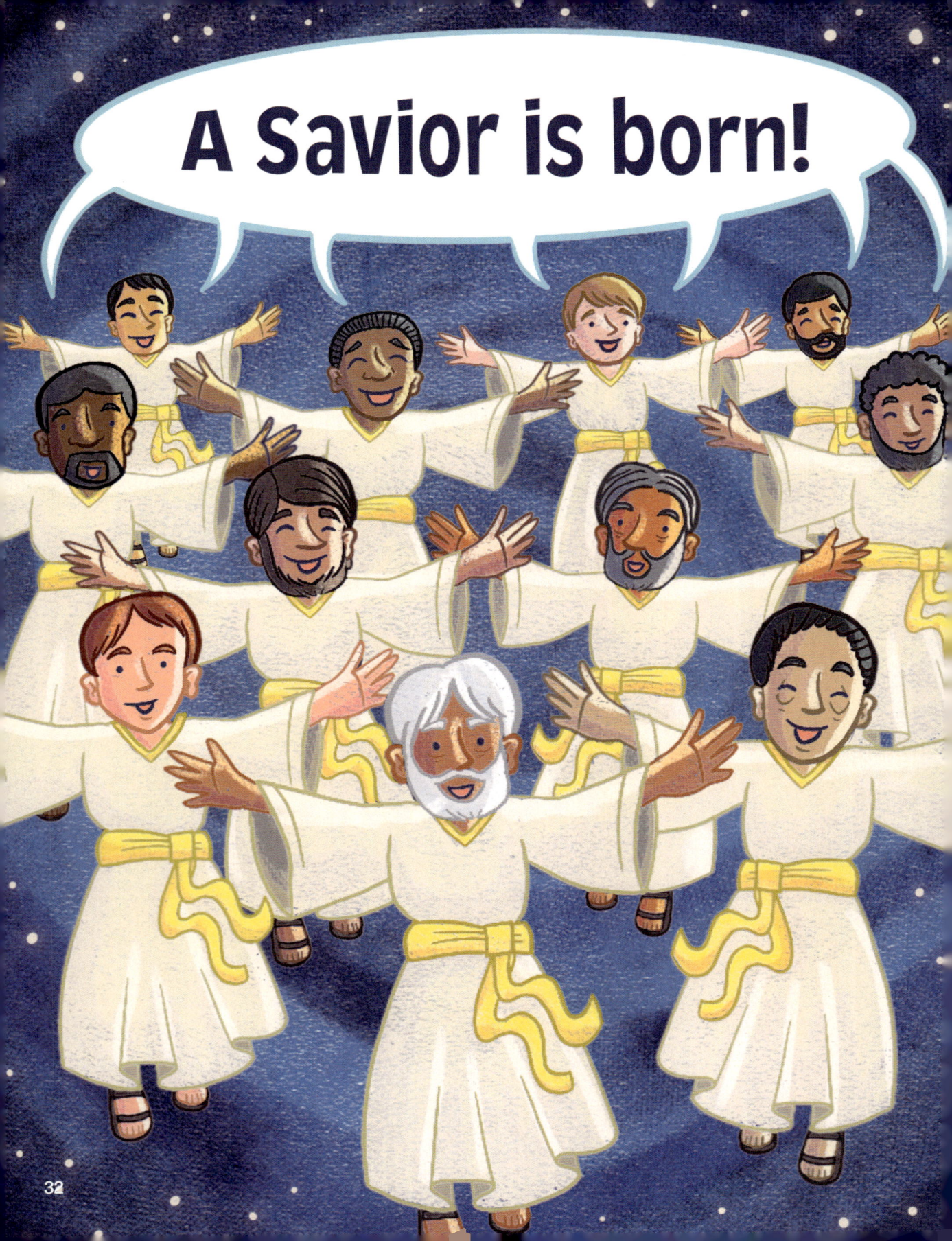

## December 15
# ANGELS AND SHEPHERDS GLORIFY AND PRAISE GOD

Suddenly, the sky was full of angels praising God! *"Glory to God in the highest, and on earth peace among those with whom he is pleased!"*

It must have been so surprising and so exciting for the shepherds to get this wonderful news! The angel had told them they would find Jesus wrapped in cloths and lying in a manger. Should they go find this special baby? Should they find this Savior born in Bethlehem? Yes! They hurried as fast as they could! And they found Mary, Joseph, and the baby...the baby in the manger wrapped in cloths. Oh, how they praised God *for all they had heard and seen!*

They had heard and seen *good news of great joy!*

---

Luke 2:13-20
Sing: "Joy to the World"

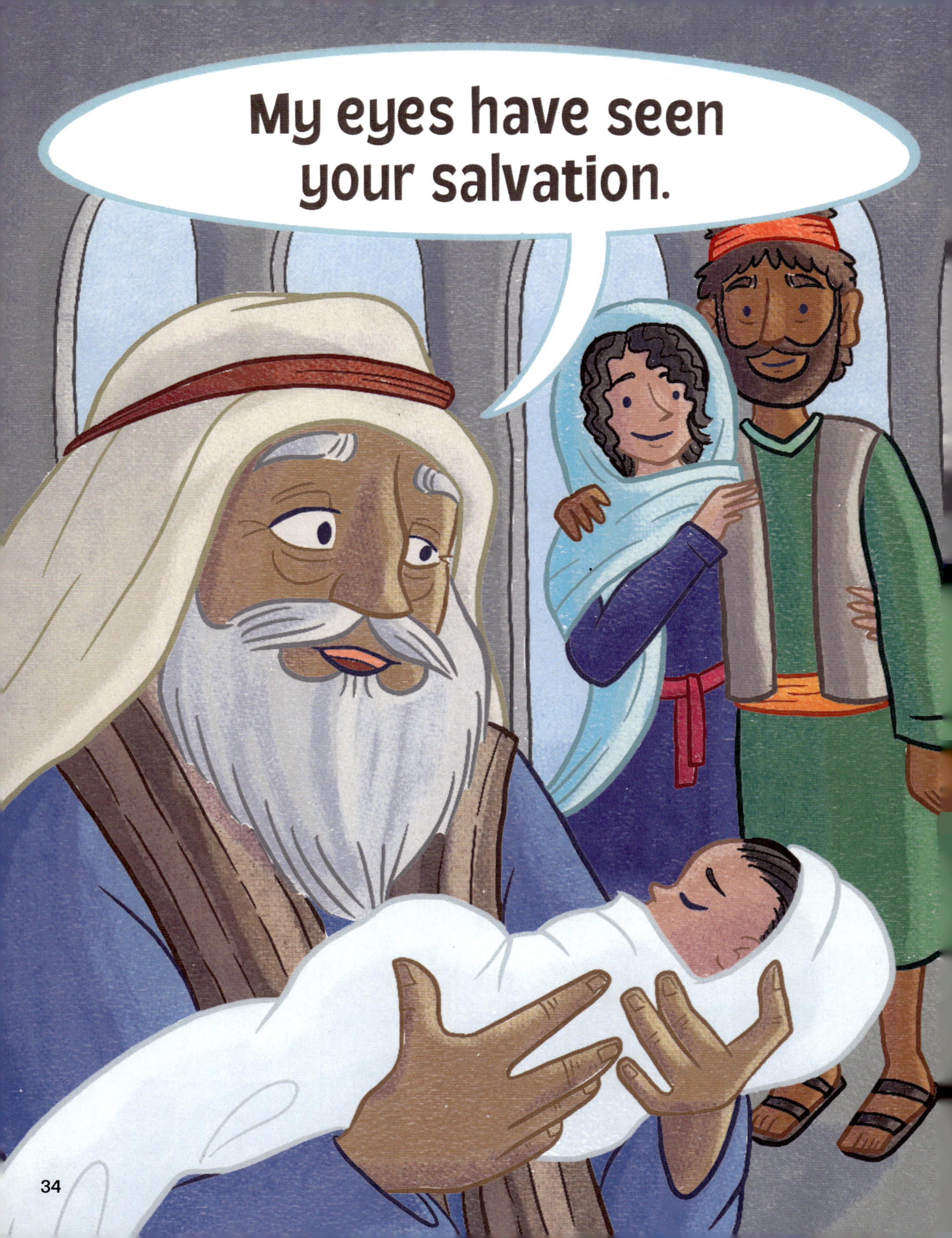
My eyes have seen your salvation.

# December 16
## Simeon Sees the Savior

Do you know who this man is? He is a priest, and his name is Simeon. Simeon had a special promise from God. God had promised that, before Simeon died, he would see the Savior. Simeon had waited so long . . . and now he was an old man. Would he see the Savior, as God had promised? Simeon had seen many people in the temple. But none of them were the Savior . . . until one day Mary and Joseph brought baby Jesus to the temple. Would Simeon know that this special baby was God's Son? Would he know that baby Jesus was the Savior?

Simeon took Jesus in his arms . . . and Simeon *knew*! And Simeon praised God! *"My eyes have seen your salvation."* Simeon could now die in peace and joy. He had seen the promised Savior! He knew that Jesus came to bring light. He came to bring brightness, truth, and joy into a world dark with sin and death.

---

Additional Reading: Luke 2:22-24
**Luke 2:25-32**

## December 17
## Wise Men Follow the Star

There were other people looking for Jesus, too. Wise men from far away had seen a special star in the sky. They knew that a special King had been born. So they followed the star to find this King.

---

Matthew 2:1-2
Sing: "We Three Kings"

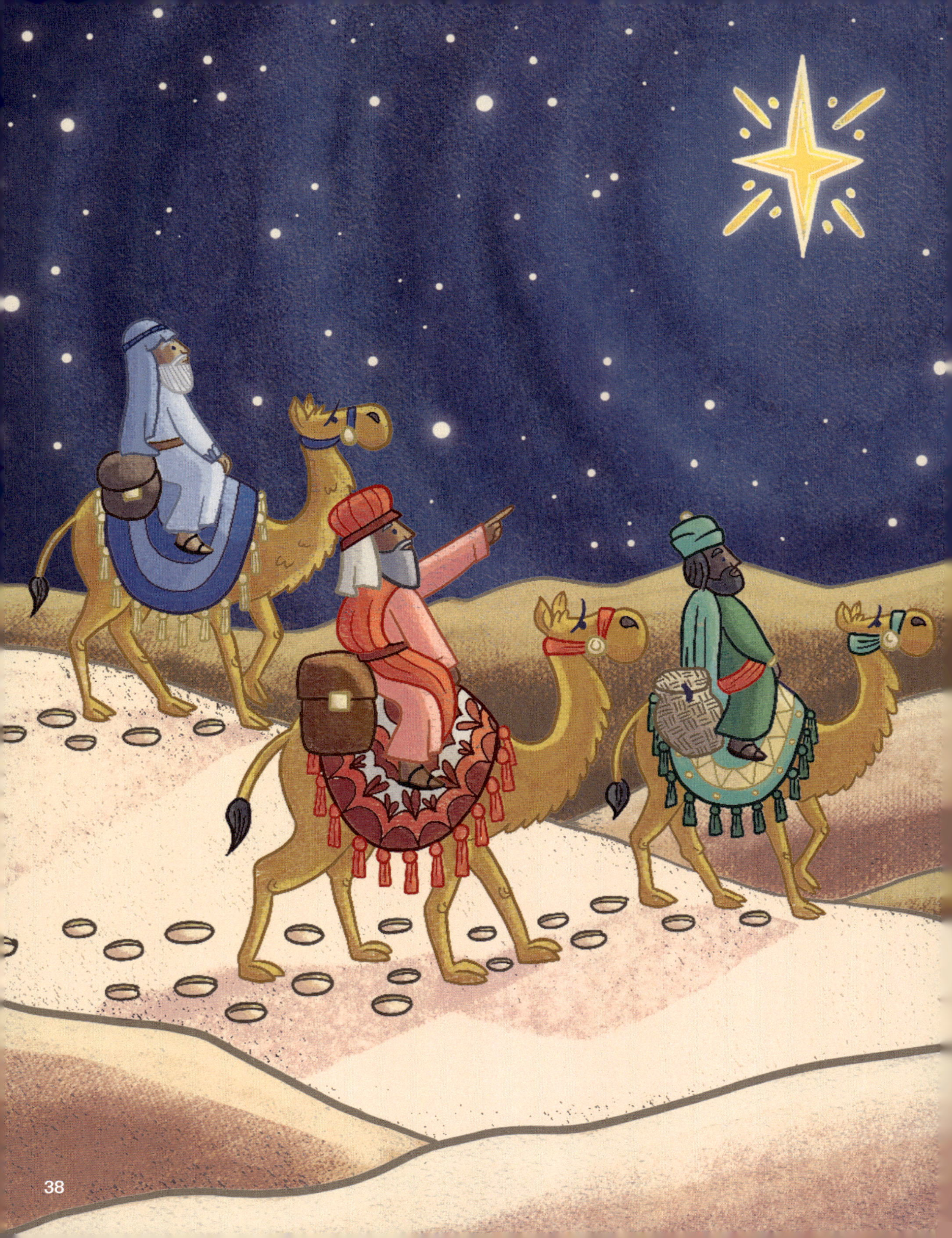

## December 18
# The Wise Men Seek the Shepherd Ruler in Bethlehem

The wise men kept following the star for many, many days... When they came to a city close to Bethlehem, they asked where they could find the special King. There was a king there named Herod. But he was not the special King. The wise men asked King Herod where they could find the special King. They wanted to worship Him.

Herod didn't know about any other king! Where was this King? Herod sent the wise men to look for Him. Herod said he wanted to worship this special King, too. But Herod lied. He really wanted to kill Jesus. But the wise men didn't know this.

---

Matthew 2:3-8

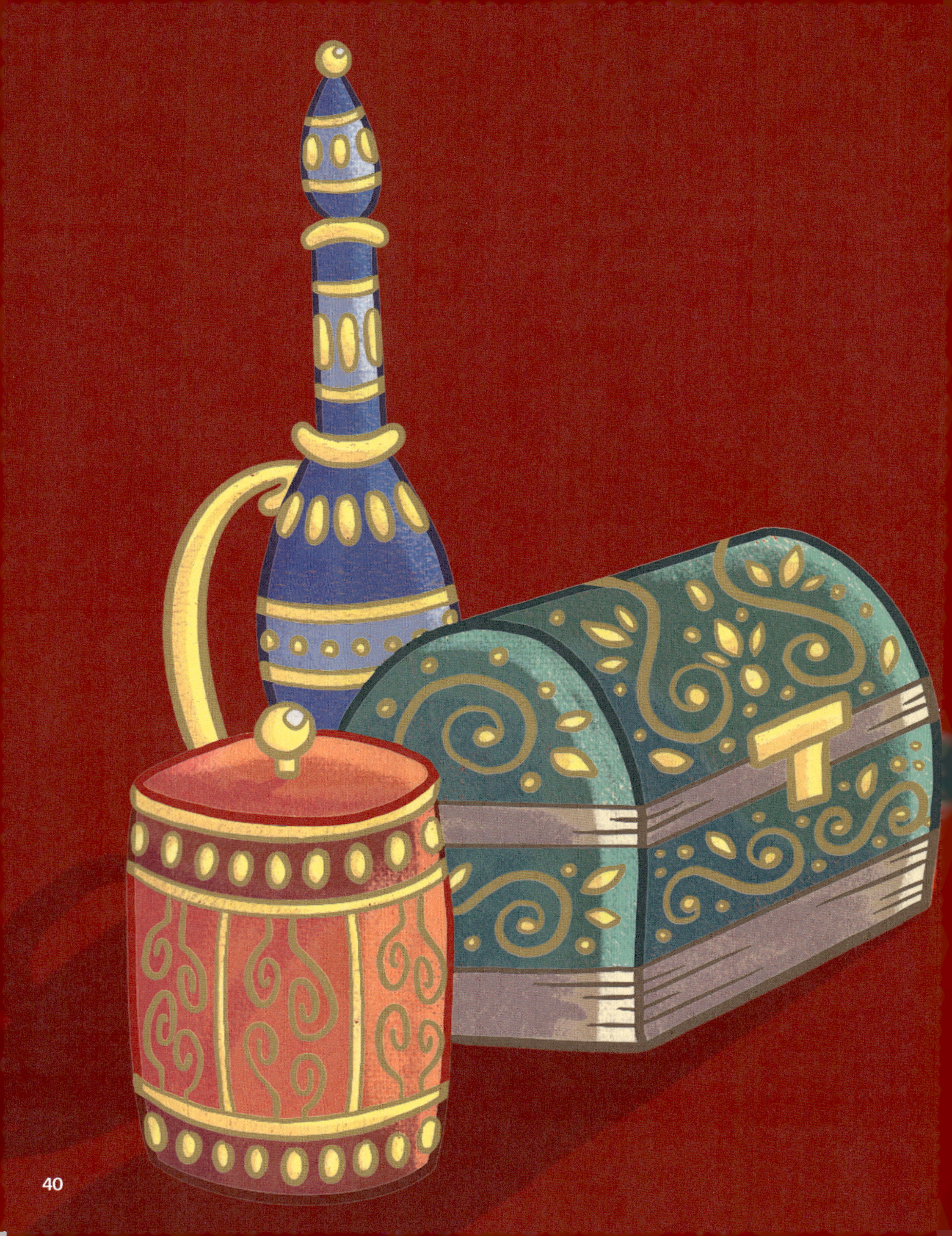

## December 19
## Gifts for the King of Kings

The wise men kept following the bright star. The star led them to Bethlehem . . . and right to the place where Jesus was. *When they saw the star, they rejoiced exceedingly with great joy.* They found the King they had been looking for! They found Jesus, God's Son! And *they fell down and worshiped him.* They had traveled so far, but they had found the Savior! They gave Him special gifts—they gave their treasures to the One who is the greatest treasure.

But they didn't tell King Herod about Jesus, who is the King of the whole world. Do you know why they didn't tell Herod? God sent an angel to warn them not to tell bad, evil King Herod about Jesus.

───────

Matthew 2:9-12

42

*December 20*

# AN ANGEL WARNS JOSEPH

God also sent an angel to Joseph in a dream. The angel told Joseph to take Mary and Jesus to the land of Egypt. So that is just what Joseph did. They left for Egypt that same night and stayed there.

---

**Matthew 2:13-15**

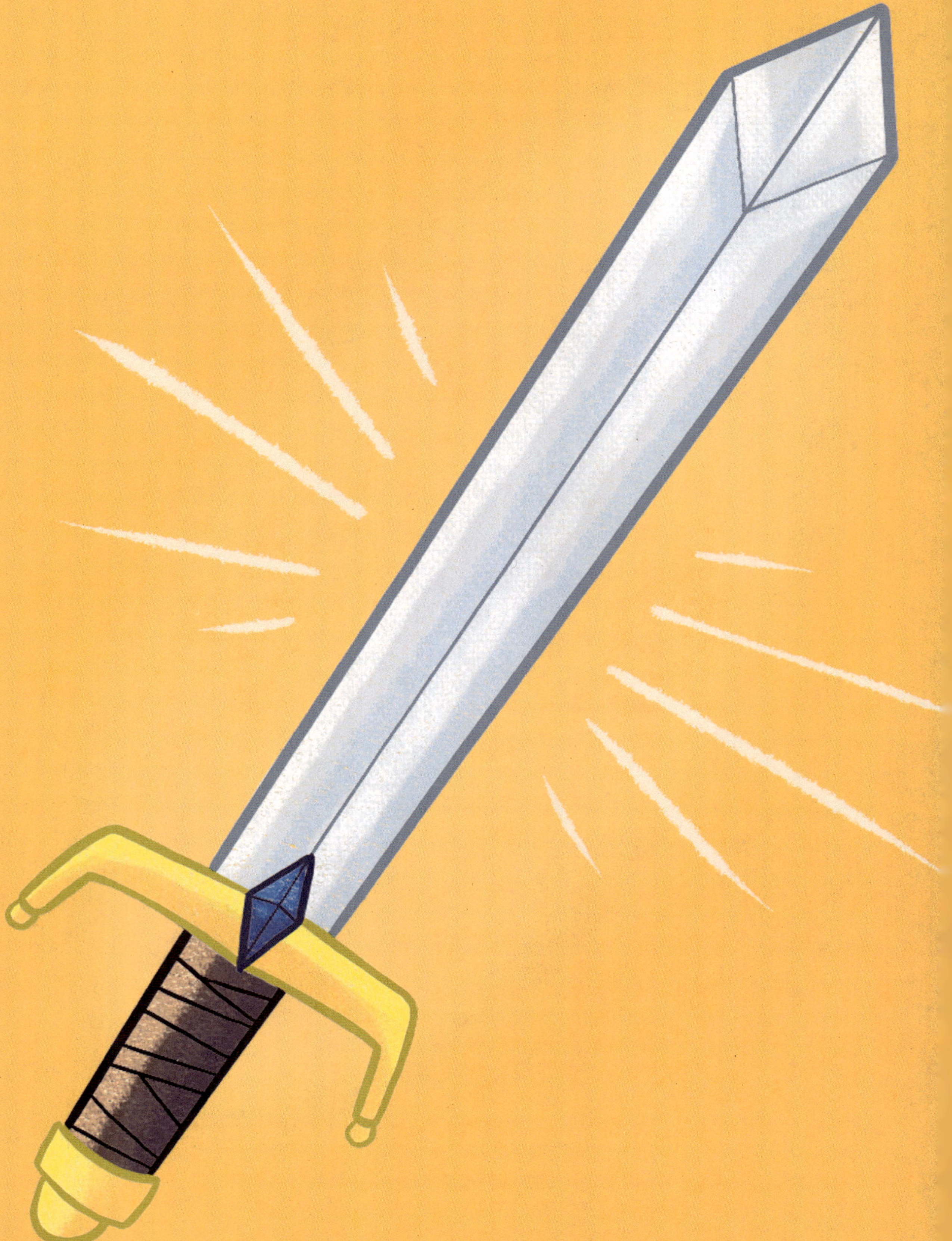

## December 21
# Jeremiah's Prophecy Fulfilled

Herod tried to kill little Jesus. He sent his soldiers with swords to kill the baby boys. But evil, awful King Herod could not kill Jesus. Jesus was safe, far away from Bethlehem.

---

**Matthew 2:16-18**

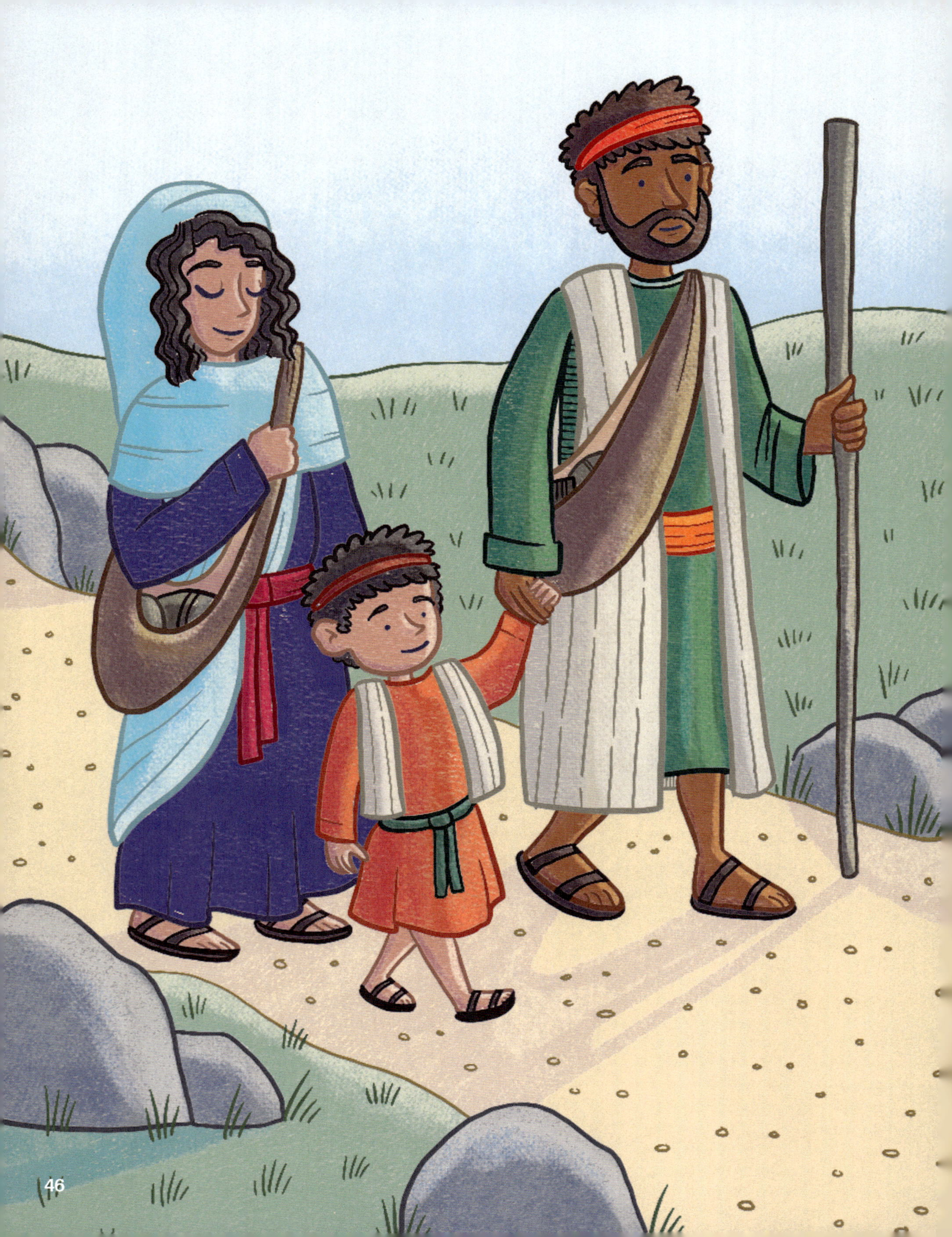

## December 22
# THE FAVOR OF GOD IS ON JESUS OF NAZARETH

How long would Joseph, Mary, and Jesus have to stay in Egypt? How would they know when it was safe to go home?

Joseph and Mary couldn't know when to go home. But God knew and, at the right time, God sent an angel to Joseph in another dream. It was now safe to go home. So, Joseph, Mary, and Jesus left Egypt and went to Nazareth. Jesus grew up in Nazareth. He became a man *filled with wisdom. And the favor of God was upon Him.*

---

Matthew 2:19-23; Luke 2:40

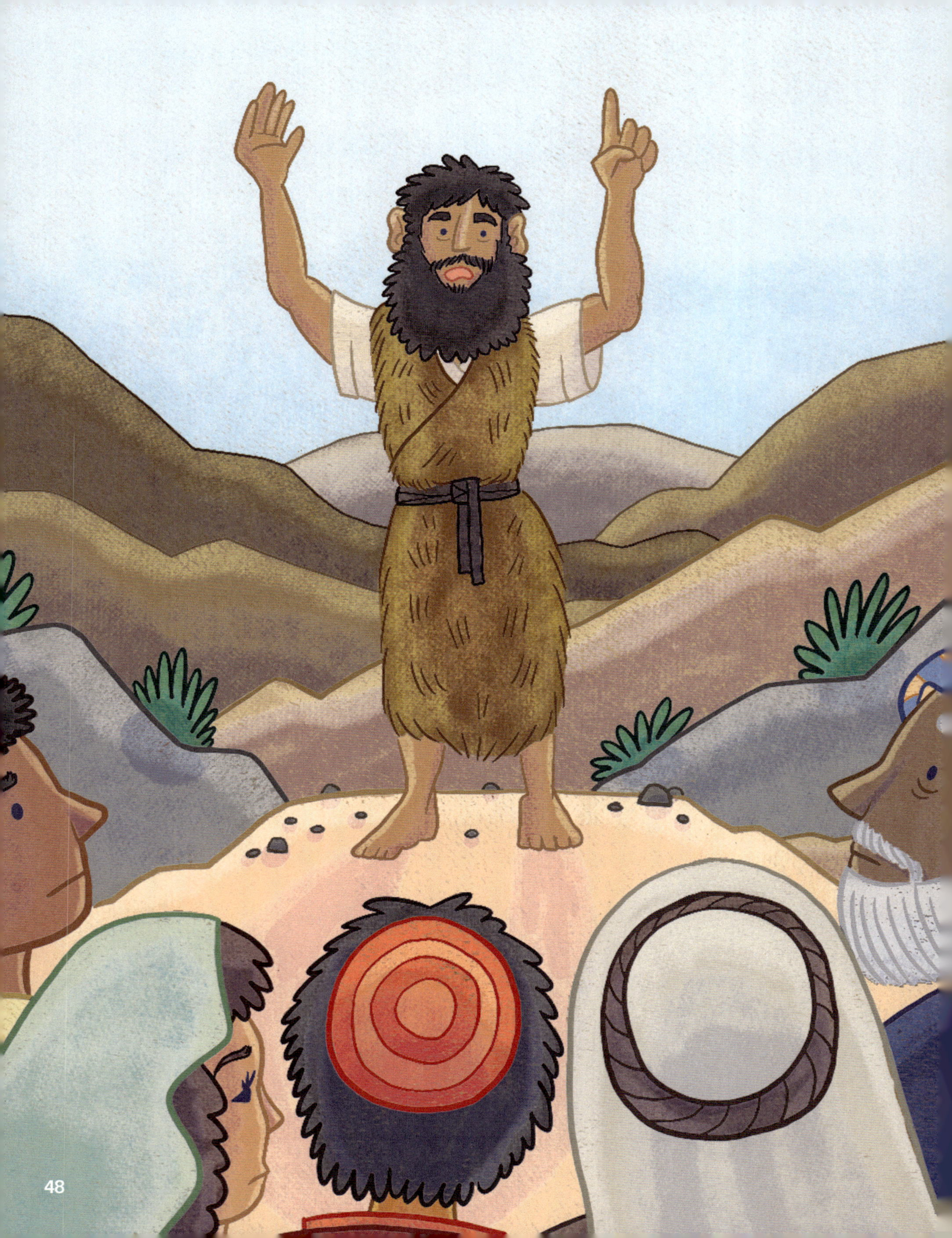

## December 23
# John the Baptist Prepares the Way of the Lord

Zechariah and Elizabeth's son, John, grew up and became a man, too. Do you remember what the angel had told Zechariah about John? He would be God's special messenger. What the angel said was true. John traveled around preaching and telling people to turn away from sin.

**Matthew 3:1-6**

# The Lamb of God

## Who takes away the sins of the world

## December 24
# Jesus, the Lamb of God

John told them about God's Son, the *very special Person*. He told them about Jesus, *who takes away the sin of the world*.

---

**John 1:29-34**
Additional Reading: John 3:16-17

RECEIVE...

BELIEVE...

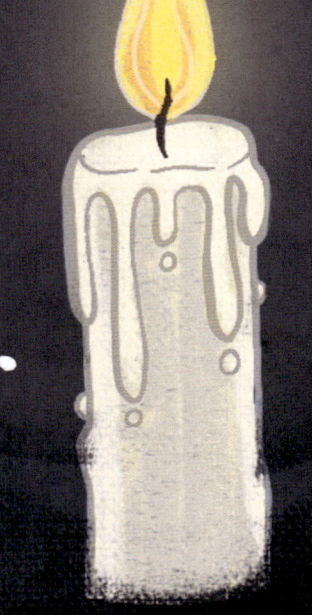

BECOME...

## December 25
# Jesus, the True Light

Why did God send His Son to earth? He sent Jesus to be a light. Have you ever been in a very dark place? When a light is turned on in the dark, it makes you happy. You can see the way to go. Jesus is the light that shows us the way to God. Jesus died on the cross so that sinners can be forgiven by God.

Everyone who welcomes Jesus and trusts Him to take away sin can be part of God's great family.

---

Additional Reading: John 1:1-5

**John 1:6-14**

# This is good news of great joy!

It is the greatest news of all!

# Truth:78

Truth78 is a vision-oriented ministry for the next generations—that they may know, honor, and treasure God, setting their hope in Christ alone, so that they will live as faithful disciples for the glory of God.

Our mission is to inspire and equip the church and the home for the comprehensive discipleship of the next generation.

We are committed to developing resources and training that are God-centered, Bible-saturated, Gospel-focused, Christ-exalting, Spirit-dependent, doctrinally grounded, and discipleship-oriented.

## Resources and Training Materials

Truth78 currently offers the following categories of resources and training materials to equip the church and home:

## Curriculum

We publish materials designed for formal Bible instruction. The scope and sequence of these materials reflects our commitment to teach children and youth the whole counsel of God over the course of their education. Materials include curricula for Sunday School, Midweek Bible programs, Backyard Bible Clubs or Vacation Bible School, and Intergenerational studies. Most of these materials can easily be adapted for use in Christian schools and education in the home.

## Vision-Casting and Training

We offer a wide variety of booklets, video and audio seminars, articles, and other practical training resources that highlight and further expound our vision, mission, and values, as well as our educational philosophy and methodology. Many of these resources are freely distributed through our website. These resources and training serve to assist ministry leaders, volunteers, and parents in implementing Truth78's vision and mission in their churches and homes.

## Parenting and Family Discipleship

We have produced a variety of materials and training designed to help parents in their role of discipling their children. These include booklets, video presentations, family devotionals, children's books, articles, and other recommended resources. Furthermore, our curricula include take-home pages to help parents apply what is taught in the classroom to their child's daily experience in order to nurture faith.

## Bible Memory

Our Fighter Verses Bible memory program is designed to encourage the church, families, and individuals in the lifelong practice and love of Bible memory. The Fighter Verses Program utilizes an easy-to-use Bible memory system with carefully chosen verses to help fight the fight of faith. There is a preschool version (Foundation Verses) for younger children with a verse pack, coloring book, and visuals packet. We also offer study and devotional guides, coloring books, and journals that correspond to the Fighter Verses.

For more information on any of these resources and training materials contact us.

Truth78.org • info@Truth78.org • (877) 400-1414

Made in the USA
Columbia, SC
25 September 2022